Mid-Hants Railway

CELEBRATING **40** YEARS IN COLOUR

Ron Neal

A proud moment for the volunteers of the Mid-Hants Railway. 'N' Class No. 31874 was re-introduced to service on the line in April 1977 following restoration from scrapyard condition ready for the re-opening of the line from Alresford to Ropley later that month. BBC South Today presenter, Bruce Parker, and his camera team are present on this important occasion. On the far right is John Bunch, owner of No. 31874, then next to him Julian (Jack) Twyman and George Reynolds who was our locomotive inspector in the early years.

Publisher - Roger Hardingham
Copyright Ron Neal &
Kingfisher Productions
ISBN 978-0-9573367-2-8
Printed in England

Published by
Kingfisher Productions
Watershed Mill, Settle
North Yorkshire, BD24 9LR
www.railwayvideo.com

Introduction

The following pages reflect on my time spent on the Mid-Hants Railway Watercress Line which I joined in the first days of preservation in 1972. All the photographs were taken by me and in colour using my trusted Praktica 35mm SLR camera.

As I have journeyed down this road I have discovered pictures I had long forgotten about. Many have been tinged with some sadness as we remember friends who are no longer with us, but have been a major part of the formation and extension of the railway up to Alton from its first 3-mile section at Ropley.

When I look at some of the work we completed at Alresford and then later at Ropley, I am amazed at the amount of tasks we covered, and to a very high standard. A lot of this work was carried out in the open air, quite often in bad weather conditions. How we did it I don't know!

I can never attempt to convey forty years of photography within one book, but maybe there will be another at some stage, who knows! I hope you enjoy this journey of 40 years of colour at the Mid-Hants Railway.

A few dedications are in order. Firstly to my long-suffering wife Chrissie who I think still understands my passion for steam engines. To my late parents, Elsie and Ralph, who pushed me in my pram along the path beside the South Western main line at Fleet, over fifty-five years ago. To see express locomotives in full flight was a sight to behold. Also thanks to them for allowing me to travel on the Hayling Island branch just before closure!

To the late Edward C. Griffiths of Farnham who sparked my interest in railway photography and who introduced me to the wonderful branch lines of mid Hampshire.

To Roger Hardingham of Kingfisher who encouraged me to produce this pictorial album.

Lastly, to all my family and friends. You have all enriched my life more than you will ever know.

Ron Neal
Bordon, Hampshire
Spring 2013

Above: The author aged 4 ½ at our old home in Albert Street, Fleet in 1957. Note the Triang train set!

Left: The author now aged 19 sitting in the 4-foot on Langstone Harbour bridge on 9th May 1971. The Hayling line had closed in November 1963.

How it all started - the early years

My own 'career' in railway preservation started by my parents taking me to the lineside at Fleet to watch the Bulleids pounding up and down the main line. I progressed on to taking a few photos at Basingstoke shed in the dying days of steam in 1967. When steam ended, I made my way to Longmoor and took more photographs and then eventually became involved at the Mid-Hants Railway.

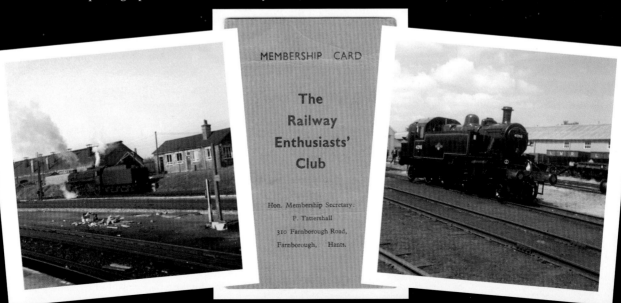

MEMBERSHIP CARD

The Railway Enthusiasts' Club

Hon. Membership Secretary:
P. Tattershall
310 Farnborough Road,
Farnborough,   Hants.

Longmoor Military Railway

A few pictures from my collection from 1970 which show some of the locomotives still at the Longmoor Military Railway at Liss. The railway was very extensive in this part of Hampshire and before the Mid-Hants line was contemplated for steam preservation, this ex-military site was the place that could have developed into a steam centre.

Top left: No. 600 *Gordon* was a 2-10-0 locomotive long associated with the military complex. It now resides at the Severn Valley Railway.

Top right: No. 75029 *The Green Knight* was purchased by David Shepherd direct from BR along with his '9F' No. 92203. No. 75029 is now owned by the North York Moors Railway.

Centre: Nos. 75029 and 92203 are seen at Liss in 1970 before they left for pastures new.

Left: No. 92203 *Black Prince* seen with its new motif on its tender.

A scene showing the second engine to arrive at the fledgling Mid-Hants line at Alresford on 18th August 1973, just seven months after British Railways closed the line. This was the start of preservation in mid Hampshire that would culminate four years later in the re-opening of the line from here to Ropley.

Left: Slough Estates No. 3 is being winched off the low-loader at Alresford. Dave Knight is seen to the left of the engine on the platform whilst Peter Dean is in the cab. See if you can spot other faces in the crowd. The other engine in the distance is a Bagnall 0-4-0ST which had arrived from Croydon 'A' power station.

Above: Pat Bell of the Permanent Way Department lines up the points at the London end of Ropley on 21st August 1976. Compare this with the scene today! Following a share issue in 1975, the railway company, then titled the Winchester & Alton Railway PLC, had been able to acquire the land all the distance to Alton, but only the track as far as Ropley. These points would enable a run-round loop to be installed so that train operations could begin.

Right: Roger Thornton, Barry Eden and Chris Bitton assemble the firebox clothing sheets on 'N' Class No. 31874 in the cattle dock at Alresford on 2nd May 1976. The locomotive was returned to steam six months later.

Above: A very historic photograph taken at Ropley on 15th May 1977. To the left is my 1970 Bond Bug three-wheeled sports car TRD 234H. Note the few items of stock, including 'West Country' Class *Bodmin* which had arrived at the railway in October 1976.

Left: 'N' Class No. 31874 at Alresford in March 1975 and seen in its short-lived livery of BR Express Passenger lined green!

Right: Our other working engine at the start of operations in 1977 was 0-6-0ST No. 196 *Errol Lonsdale*. This had arrived at the railway in late 1976 from the Kent & East Sussex Railway but was originally used on the Longmoor Military Railway until 1969. No. 196 was quickly prepared ready to assist No. 31874 in the first passenger train operations.

No. 196 is seen running round its train at Ropley on 15th May 1977.

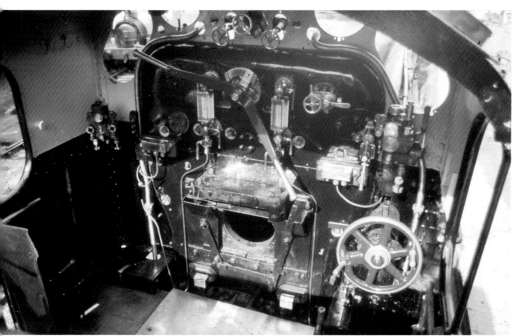

Left: The sparkling cab interior on newly restored 'N' Class No. 31874. Taken in August 1976 shortly before the locomotive returned to steam.

The Southern 'N' Class was a right-hand drive locomotive. The regulator arm is seen as is the reverser equipment on the lower right-hand side of the photograph.

Above and left: Our first main line locomotive overhaul was nearly complete in this photograph taken on 12th September 1976. Final paintwork was being completed including some lining out. The engine carried the name of *Aznar Line* in recognition of the shipping company that sponsored the move of the locomotive from Barry scrapyard.

Left: By 31st October 1976 No. 31874 had been steamed and it was ready to receive the final lining out of the cab sides, here being undertaken by Nigel Smith

Above: By 1976 other main line locomotives started to arrive. 'West Country' Class No. 34016 *Bodmin* is seen soon after delivery to Alresford on 31st October 1976. The locomotive had departed from Barry scrapyard in 1972 initially for Quainton Road, but then re-located to the MHR.

Right: 'U' Class No. 31806 had also arrived at Alresford in late October 1976. This engine was formerly a 'River' 'K' Class 2-6-2T locomotive, No. A806 *River Torridge* but rebuilt in 1928 following an accident at Sevenoaks to classmate No. A800 *River Cray*.

Above: One of the powerful LSWR Urie designed 4-6-0s arrived in April 1976. No. 30506 was purchased via a fund-raising appeal by the Urie Locomotive Society which began in 1972. Following a vote by its membership in 1975, it was agreed to bring No. 30506 to the MHR. After a short period in the cattle dock at Alresford the locomotive was moved to this location next to the old goods shed in March 1977.

Left: The S15 points towards the west at Alresford and to the track that was lifted by BR between here, Itchen Abbas and Winchester junction.

No. 31874 is prepared at Alresford for its first proving run to Ropley. Ron Hack, Julian (Jack) Twyman are seen by the front of the engine with John Bunch and Barry Eden in the cab. Opportunity was taken to move 'S15' No. 30506 up to Ropley on the same day, 3rd April 1977, in readiness for the railway to start operating later in the month.

Above and left: 'N' Class No. 31874 is seen running round its three carriages at Ropley during its test runs on 3rd April 1977. This also helped to 'prove' the trackwork prior to inspection and re-opening of the line.

Right top: No. 31874 runs light down the grade towards Alresford from Ropley. At this time the tender was still to receive its final lining and BR emblem.

Right bottom: Nos. 196 and 31874 in the loop at Ropley. These two locomotives would perform the mainstay of operations until the emergence of *Bodmin* two years later.

Right: Slough Estates No. 3 is lit up by television engineers in early 1975 as part of a live programme broadcast from the railway on the local BBC channel.

Left: During the same evening Mid-Hants volunteers are seen enjoying themselves with a rare Alvis car showroom light box. The chap in the red hat is Richard Audsley who was one of the leading volunteers in the early days. To his immediate left is Steve Ryder and to his right we see Steve Bell, John Elliot and Mike Smith.

Above: 'U' Class 31806 stored in a line of stock at Ropley in May 1977. Restoration of 31806 would wait until No. 34016 *Bodmin* was completed in 1979. In the event the 'U' took just 18 months to restore from scrapyard condition returning to steam in April 1981.

Right: 'West Country' Class No. 34016 *Bodmin* at Ropley awaiting restoration. By this time, in May 1977, the locomotive had received some restoration work, mostly whilst at Quainton Road. It would steam in just two years from this point!

Without any covered accommodation in those early years, the restoration team on *Bodmin* erected a polythene tent with a framework made up from old boiler smoke tubes. This at least allowed work to continue in all weathers. No. 34016 was the first rebuilt Bulleid light pacific to be rescued from Woodhams yard at Barry. Soon the locomotive would be ready and become the flagship engine of the Mid-Hants Railway - putting the line really on the map!

Above left: The centre big end on *Bodmin*'s driving wheel. The device shown in the middle is an 'Ecob' hand-cranked turning tool. This was used over an 18-month period to skim the metal surface of the journals. We took out a 0.140″ score on the journal to leave its final diameter to within 0.003″ of ovality!

Above right: The 'West Country' Class takes shape within the makeshift tent at Ropley.

By Easter (April 1979) only the lamps to be wired up and a final coat of paint.

Above: Steam test and final work is completed on *Bodmin*, No. 31874 continues to operate the railway's services. Just two years after re-opening, the Mid-Hants Railway was a great success and was pulling in the crowds - soon becoming one of Hampshire's main tourist attractions.

Right: With its final coat of BR brunswick green applied, all that was needed was the fitting of the cabside numbers and tender lining. Nameplates would be fitted ready for the re-naming ceremony at Alresford in September 1979 by the mayor of Bodmin in Cornwall who made the journey to Hampshire especially.

By late August 1979 No. 34016 *Bodmin* was ready to start her test runs. Without nameplates, the locomotive is seen running round a set of carriages at Ropley in early September 1979. We were blessed with glorious weather all week and the tests were all successful. I was very proud to have been part of the team restoring this magnificent locomotive from scrapyard condition. It became the first Bulleid from Barry to be restored to service and inspired others to do the same.

A very proud moment for me. The author on the footplate of 'N' Class No. 31874 at Ropley having just passed his drivers exam under the guidance of Senior Locomotive Inspector George Reynolds. George was very much a 'southern' man and was a crucial part in our first days of getting the railway open. He was a driver during the locomotive exchanges of 1948. Picture taken on my Praktica camera by Andy Crespin who now lives in New Zealand. 31st August 1980.

Another footplate shot, this time on *Bodmin* in the yard at Ropley on 21st August 1981. The locomotive is in its usual immaculate condition, thanks to the sterling efforts of Matt Hawkesly, another one of our early volunteers who is sadly no longer with us.

By now, 29th August 1981, we had a nice covered shed at Ropley where we could all work in relative comfort. No. 31874 is having a 'bottom end' mechanical overhaul, after four years hard service since reopening in 1977.

Above: Dick Woodruff, left, and Alan Grenig pose for me on the footplate of 'U' Class 31806 in Ropley yard on 20th March 1982. This shot was inspired by those taken by Edward Griffiths on the Meon Valley line during the late 1940s. It's a nice period shot of a timeless scene. Dick sadly passed away several years ago.

Left: A mid-week photograph of No. 31874 on a permanent way train on 11th June 1982. The extension of the line towards Medstead & Four Marks was in progress at this time and many trains were being propelled towards the extension railhead.

Above: 'U' Class No. 31806 is seen between Ropley and Alresford on a down train in August 1982. At this time we ran with a rake of suburban coaches with a 'BY' van attached at one end. Driver on this occasion was Dave Knight.

Right: I get a friendly wave from Fireman Harry Usmar as he passes by on the footplate of *Bodmin* in August 1982.

Above: No. 34016 *Bodmin* in the run-round loop at Ropley during a Gala event on 4th April 1983. Mike Berry's original 'ACE' headboard adorns the smokebox.

Left: Peter Cutler, Syd Weaver and Dick Pate pose on the footplate of *Bodmin* during the same Gala.

The author leaning on No. 31874 waiting for his next duty on 4th April 1983. The idyllic Hampshire station at Ropley was getting more attention following years of neglect in BR times. The famous topiary on the down side was being maintained well and much renovation work on the station buildings being undertaken.
This photograph was taken with my camera, but by my regular fireman at the time, Matt Hawkesly.
Note the North Cornwall headcode!

LSWR 'T9' Class No. 30120 in its recently restored state at Ropley in the company of No. 31874 on 18th May 1983. This unique engine was restored by the Urie Locomotive Society who arranged a loan for several years from the National Railway Museum at York where it had been in store for many years.

No. 30120 was reserved for the national collection upon withdrawal in 1961. The locomotive entered Eastleigh Works and was restored to a light green LSWR livery. 20 years later, the engine emerged from Ropley shed in this early BR livery.

In May 1983 the railway extended its operations as far as Medstead & Four Marks, about three miles further east from Ropley. The volunteers had set this goal in 1980 and they achieved it. It would be a further two years before the line was further extended onto Alton itself, therefore accomplishing the original aims of the railway in 1975.

'U' Class No. 31806 arrives at the delightful station of Medstead on 14th June 1983. The crew are Fireman Duncan Marchant and Driver Dave Bailey.

The railway's latest addition to its fleet of locomotives arrives at Medstead on 14th June 1983. 'T9' No. 30120 looks resplendent in its BR livery with the early BR small emblem on its tender. The class would have been seen regularly over the Mid-Hants route in the 1920 and 30s.

With fresh ballast and re-used track, the station is in business again, although just out of sight to the right of the left-hand picture, the railway was still seeing considerable tracklaying towards Alton. The engine would be detached here and run-round for a return to Ropley and Alresford.

Above: Another of my favourite photographs. 'U' Class No. 31806 and 'N' Class No. 31874 coupled tender to tender bring an 8-coach special up the bank near Bishop's Sutton towards Ropley. It is about 3.30pm and the low autumn light shines well on the two locomotives and train.

Right: The 'T9' heads tender first down towards Alresford on 23rd October 1983. The photograph shows the lines of the tender to good effect here which is an 8-wheeled Drummond type.

November 1983 and the second of the Urie S15s at Barry is delivered to the cattle dock at Alresford for eventual use on the railway. No. 30499 was purchased by the Urie Locomotive Society in early 1983 to achieve the aim of owning both remaining examples for preservation. No. 30499 was built at Eastleigh Works in May 1920 and is as such the oldest surviving locomotive built at Eastleigh.

0-6-0ST No. 196 *Errol Lonsdale* prepares to shunt the S15 ready for its journey to Ropley.

Work on restoring No. 30499 to working order was underway at the time of writing (Winter 2012).

Above: No. 34016 *Bodmin* brings a nice set of 'blood and custard' Mk1 coaches down the grade at Soldridge, near Four Marks in April 1984.

Right: Yet another addition to the fleet of locomotives at the Mid-Hants Railway entered service in 1984. BR Standard Class 2-6-0 No. 76017 had left Barry scrapyard in January 1974 initially to Quainton Road, Buckinghamshire but then removed to the MHR in 1978 for restoration.

Above: Standard Class 4 No. 76017 was built in June 1953 and after just 12 years in service, withdrawn and sent to Barry in South Wales. Driver Frank Howells is ready to do business on this day in May 1984.

Left: The popular 2-6-0 locomotive was the fourth 'Barry' engine to be completely restored by volunteers at the railway by 1984 with two more on their way to completion for 1987 - Nos. 30506 and 34105 *Swanage*.

Above: Pioneering MHR locomotive No. 31874 runs round its train at Medstead & Four Marks. Within a year the engine would be able to take its train all the distance to Alton.

Right: A scene of the shed area at Ropley in 1984. *Bodmin* negotiates the shed entrance line as three other locomotives wait for their turn.

The tranquil setting of Alresford's eastern end as Standard Class 4 No. 76017 is readied to take its service towards Ropley on a hot summer's day in August 1984. My fireman brings coal forward on the tender ready for the journey. The signals at Alresford have now been altered to LSWR lower quadrant types.

Somerset & Dorset Reunion

Two famous figures from the Somerset & Dorset line's history appear at a special Gala at the MHR to commemorate the anniversary of the last 'Pines' Express over the S&D on 8th September 1962. On 8th September 1984, legendary driver Donald Beale takes the regulator of *Bodmin*. Donald was a driver at Bath and Branksome during his long career. On the right is Donald's regular fireman, Peter Smith, who is enjoying a ride aboard Standard Class 4 No. 76017. Peter drove No. 92220 *Evening Star* on the final up 'Pines' in 1962.

Above and below: The winter following the S&D Gala of 1984 and the extension to Alton is well underway. A new Crawler crane is being tested in January 1985 in the Chawton Woods area. This Hudswell Clarke diesel shunter was on loan from the BP Oil terminal at Hamble. In just five months the line was opened to Alton in May 1985!

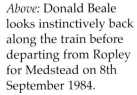

Above: Donald Beale looks instinctively back along the train before departing from Ropley for Medstead on 8th September 1984.

'T9' No. 30120 makes a spirited start away from Ropley with No. 31806 behind its tender in March 1985. With high water levels inside the 'T9s' boiler the drain cocks remained open!

Above: 'West Country' Class pacific No. 34105 *Swanage* under restoration inside Ropley's works in April 1985. By now the locomotive is well underway and would be steamed by August 1987.

Left: Wayne Tallon works on the frames of a WD 2-10-0 that came from Greece. Work progresses in the shed in April 1985.

Right: As work progressed on *Swanage*, some restoration was taking place on 'Merchant Navy' Class No. 35018 *British India Line*. The 'Merchant' had arrived at the railway from Barry in March 1980.

Below: Railway 'flagship' engine *Bodmin* in the yard at Ropley with Nos. 76017, 30120 and 31874 in 1986.

Above: The Standard Class 4 No. 76017 is sandwiched between *Bodmin* and the 'T9' at Ropley shed. The line had just been extended to Alton during this year, 1985, and a good fleet of locomotives was essential.

Left: A close-up of *Bodmin*. By this time, May 1985, the 'West Country' had been in service some six years.

Above: One of the Sunday gangs of volunteers on the up-side bank at Ropley. It was not uncommon to have over 100 people on site, especially on Sundays! Can you spot yourself or a friend here?

Right: Further scenes around the shed yard at Ropley showing the locomotive fleet at the time - May 1985.

Above and right: Andy Crespin carefully drives Sentinel diesel No. 610 *General Lord Robertson* off the low loader at Alresford in May 1985. Martin Buckle and Frank Howells are present.

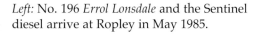

Left: No. 196 *Errol Lonsdale* and the Sentinel diesel arrive at Ropley in May 1985.

Former Feltham engineman, Roy Davis, leans out of *Bodmin*'s cab as they round the curve at Mount Pleasant Bridge near Alton on a very hot summer's day in June 1985.

Above: The 'Greek' 2-10-0 outshopped at Ropley in May 1986. It was given the fictitious number of 90775. The locomotive was soon sold to the North Yorkshire Moors Railway and left the Mid-Hants for good.

Left: The hulk of locomotive BR Standard Class 5 No. 73096 awaits completion at Ropley.

The two Maunsell Moguls pass at Medstead & Four Marks station in May 1987. 'U' Class No. 31806 arrives from Ropley as No. 31874 is ready to depart once the single line token has been exchanged.

Above: 'West Country' Class Pacific No. 34105 *Swanage* inside the shed at Ropley in June 1987 and nearly ready to roll. My toolbox and bag are on the ground beneath the cab. The loco and tender were both spray-painted to a very high finish.

Left: No. 34105 *Swanage* at Ropley being tested prior to its naming ceremony. Driver Tom Turner is seen oiling round and making sure all is well.

Right: Always a memorable moment for any newly outshopped locomotive. *Swanage* is re-named by the mayor of Swanage on 26th August 1987.

Below: Newly re-named 'West Country' Class *Swanage* climbs up to Ropley near Bishop's Sutton on her way to Alton in September 1987.

The familiar flat sided boiler casing on the un-rebuilt Bulleid Pacifics is seen to good effect here. This all had to be made from new during the restoration of No. 34105 *Swanage*. August 1987.

Another favourite shot of mine taken at Medstead in September 1987. I took this picture during a lay-over at the station. I was driving the 'T9' N. 30120 and managed to get time to push the camera button. The train engine was of course No. 34105 *Swanage*. This period was a bit of a heyday one for the Mid-Hants railway. We were running all the way from Alresford to Alton and we had a good stock of locomotives to choose from.

Right: Urie 'S15' No. 30506 was re-dedicated into service on the same day as 'West Country' Class *Swanage* on 26th August 1987. No. 506 had entered service on 8th July. The engine hauls a train between Ropley and Alresford in April 1988. The Urie Society painted the engine in full Southern green livery and with the number '506'.

Below: A down train climbing past the shrave on its way to Medstead & Four Marks.

Remembering the 'M7' period

You cannot do a pictorial album about the Mid-Hants Railway without a mention of the Drummond 'M7' Class. These engines were commonly seen on the line between Alton and Winchester up until 1957 as they operated the 'push-pull' services calling at Medstead, Ropley, Alresford and Itchen Abbas before joining the main London to Southampton line at Winchester Junction.

In 1993 the only working example, No. 30053, was loaned for a spell on the MHR courtesy of the Drummond Locomotive Society based at the Swanage Railway. At this time, No. 30053 was being used on the main line too.

In 2012 the 'M7' was to visit the line again. This time it was painted in Southern wartime black livery with sunshine lettering as No. 53.

The 'M7s' worked the 'push-pull' trains for over 20 years before, in 1957, the line received the then new DEMU units which were taking over many rural services in Hampshire.

A special event was planned in May 1988 to celebrate 150 years of the railway arriving at Woking. 'Our' 'T9' No. 120, by now re-painted in Southern green livery, was taken by road to be exhibited there. What a splendid sight she made during the day and at night with yard lighting on her. The whole event was a great success.

Taken from the former North Tawton footbridge, now at Ropley, No. 120 pilots No. 506 towards Alresford in June 1988. Both locomotive's were restored back to operational use by the Urie Locomotive Society and other MHR volunteers.

Driver Alan Campling brings No. 506 over the Butts Junction site before tackling the 1 in 60 gradient to Medstead. One injector will already be on and the fireman will be busy with his shovel! This point in the line was once a junction with a line to the north to Basingstoke and another line travelled south along the Meon Valley route to Fareham. Both lines closed very early on, with the Basingstoke branch closing in September 1932 and the Meon Valley closing in February 1955 to passenger traffic. Butts Junction signalbox was abolished in February 1935.

Each year we try and remember the sad day in July 1967 when steam traction finally ceased on the Southern Region of BR. It was the last main line steam route in Britain. We see Andy Crespin's headboard attached to the front of *Swanage*. My regular fireman at this time in July 1988 was Ricky Pallett, an ex-Fratton engineman who sadly is also no longer with us.

Left: Swanage brings an up train through the 'shrave' on its way from Medstead to Alton in May 1989.

Above: 'West Country' Class 4-6-2 No. 34016 *Bodmin* catches the last rays of sunlight at Alresford during a Santa Special day in December 1988.

Right: Platform 2 at Alton with 'T9' No. 120 piloting Urie 'S15' No. 506 during the summer Gala of 1989..

Above: Preserved 4-Sub Electric Unit alongside 'S15' No. 506 at Alton' Platform 2 during the July 1989 Gala. The 4-Sub had been running shuttles to and from Woking. I was driver of No. 506 that day.

Left: 'T9' No. 120 by now in its Southern green waits for the road at Alton. The MHR had a special agreement with BR to use this platform in those days. Trains no longer use the main Network Rail platforms at Alton, so these are very rare pictures.

Above: 'U' Class No. 31806 pilots Standard Class 4 No. 76017 into Alton station in July 1989.

Right: 'S15' No. 506 at the head of a cavalcade of locomotives at Medstead in July 1989. Behind No. 506 are Nos. 120, 76017 and 31806. We had nine of our own locomotives in service that day with four pairs double-heading!

Above: 'T9' No. 120 shows its Southern green off well here with gold lettering on its tender. No. 506 is in a similar livery. They are on the down side at Ropley station.

Right: 'West Country' Class No. 34105 *Swanage* climbing up to Ropley on a Santa Special in December 1989. She is running with a tender formerly attached to No. 35018 *British India Line*.

From Woodhams' yard at Barry, South Wales To Alresford, Hampshire

Many readers may not realise that most of the locomotives at the Mid-Hants Railway came from a scrapyard at Barry in South Glamorgan. Woodham Bros. yard at Barry started accumulating redundant steam locomotives from the late 1950s through to 1968 - the end of steam in Britain. Many Southern Region engines were purchased for scrap and made their way to Barry to be cut up. By chance Dai Woodham, owner of the scrapyard, decided to concentrate on other scrapping of wagons and carriages, leaving the locomotives until the end. By the time steam finished in 1968, preservationists from all over Britain persuaded Woodhams to sell the locomotives to them for various fledgling railway schemes, including the one in mid Hampshire. And so the Mid-Hants started to acquire locomotives from Barry via private owners or societies. In total 16 locomotives arrived by road at Alresford for eventual use. The largest number to any preserved line in Britain. The following pages illustrate just a few of the engines still in their scrapyard environment before departure for Hampshire.

Left: 'Battle of Britain' Class Pacific No. 34067 *Tangmere* at Barry scrapyard in August 1975. Many of the locomotives were by now getting into very poor external condition after many years in the open and close to the sea.

Tangmere went to Alresford in January 1981 and then departed from the MHR to be overhauled to main line condition at Swindon then Bury.

Right: 'N' Class No. 31874 in the top yard at Barry in July 1970. Many of the elderly Southern locomotives to arrive at Barry were stored in this area, including the 'S15's and 'Us'. The engine was brought to the Mid-Hants in 1974 and was steamed again in October 1976.

Above: 'U' Class No. 31806 in the lower yard at Barry in August 1975. We had given it a lick of paint just to make it look more presentable.

Below left: 'Battle of Britain' Class No. 34073 *249 Squadron*. Like many of the Bulleids, No. 34073 had lost its tender due to them being sold off to a steel works in the late 1960s.

Below right: 'Merchant Navy' Class No. 35018 *British India Line* awaits preservation in 1970. This locomotive was the first of the Bulleids to be rebuilt at Eastleigh from original condition in 1956.

Above: Standard Class '5' No. 73096 in the Chawton Woods area near to Medstead in February 1996.

Left: BR Standard Class '9F' No. 92203 *Black Prince* just west of Ropley in February 1996.

Gresley 'A4' Pacific No. 60007 *Sir Nigel Gresley* cruises past Hampshire Hunt in April 1996. The famous locomotive visited the MHR for a period on loan from its base at the North York Moors Railway.

Above: The un-familiar lines of an 'A4' in the Hampshire countryside. No. 60007 *Sir Nigel Gresley* makes a colourful sight as it plies the line between Medstead and Ropley in May 1996 during its stay on the railway.

Left: The 'A4' is seen on its approach to the A31 road bridge prior to arrival at Alresford in May 1996.

Above: Another 'A4' Pacific arrived at the railway in the late 1990s. No. 60019 *Bittern* came to Ropley for an overhaul following purchase by its new owner, Jeremy Hosking. Once restored, *Bittern* was used on the line and on main line railtours. It is now based at Southall.

Right: Stand Class '5' No. 73096 attacks the bank towards Medstead. The locomotive was brought to the railway in July 1985 and was first steamed in July 1993 before a further overhaul took it on to the main line as well as Mid-Hants services.

Above: 'S15' No. 506 in April 1990. Driver Barry Stratton looks back down the train to ensure all is well. The train is in the 'shrave' near Medstead which is on the incline of 1 in 60 grade at this point. The pressure gauge needle is right over, so she's on the boil!

Left: No. 506 on a down train near Bishop's Sutton. Springtime in Hampshire - April 1990.

Opposite page: No. 34105 *Swanage* runs down the bank with Matthew Hawksley's headboard of the 'Atlantic Coast Express' on the smokebox door.

Left: One of the engines repatriated from Greece in 1984. This is American-built 'S160' Class WD701 *Franklin D Roosevelt* seen on the line near Medstead on its first passenger train duty.

Below: The 'S160' sits on Ropley shed in May 1990. The striking livery was copied from the Longmoor Military Railway's colours. This railway was close-by in Hampshire but closed in 1969.

In April 1993 a visit was made by 'Battle of Britain' Class No. 34072 *257 Squadron* from the Swanage Railway. Piloting our own un-rebuilt Bulleid *Swanage*, the pair descend the grade between Ropley and Alresford. It was a rare sight seeing two un-rebuilt Bulleid Pacifics double-heading. A return favour was made to the Swanage Railway with No. 34105 *Swanage* travelling to the Dorset line.

Above: Maunsell 'S15' No. 828 is now resident at the Mid-Hants. In 1993 it was used on the main line following restoration at the Eastleigh Works site under the guidance of former Erecting Shop Foreman Harry Frith. The engine is seen at Salisbury in October 1993 in the company of pioneer 'Britannia' No. 70000 *Britannia.*

Left: No. 828 paired with 'King Arthur' Class No. 30777 *Sir Lamiel* up Liss bank on 1st April 1995 - the first day of privatisation on British Rail!

Captain John Treasure-Jones retired, proudly holds a replica headboard of the famous Boat Train 'The Cunarder' on the front of 'West Country' Class *Bodmin* . Ian Dean, left, was General Manager of the MHR at the time. John Treasure-Jones was the last captain of Cunard's RMS *Queen Mary* and had the task of delivering the liner in October 1967 to its new home at Long Beach, California. My favourite of all liners.

'The Cunarder' Boat Train

With the right lighting available, night-time shots can be effective. Here, No.34105 *Swanage* is seen at Ropley on 1st December 1990. No. 76017 is in front of the 'West Country' Class Pacific.

Above: A calm winter evening at gas lit Alresford station with Standard Class 4 No. 76017 ready to depart with one of the popular Santa Specials.

Left: No. 76017 on shed at Ropley following a long day driving on the footplate. December 1990.

Above: To show what 'Battle of Britain' Class *Tangmere* might look like when restored, No. 34105 *Swanage* was 'dressed' up as *Tangmere* in April 1991. Matthew Hawksley leans out of the cab.

Left: WD Nos. 601 and 701 at Ropley in August 1991. For all the world it could be a depot scene at the Longmoor Military Railway.

Above: John Rooney at the controls as No. 34105 *Swanage* is in full flight down the grade. This photograph shows the tender to good effect and the raves of the tank side. This tender was formed from a new tank on a base of a long bodied 'Merchant Navy' Class chassis.

Right: Nos. 31874 and 31625 on shed at Ropley. No. 31625 had been restored to service in 1997.

On the main line

Left: Frimley Junction at 15.50hrs on 20th February 1997. We see 'U' Class No. 31625 on its test run prior to acceptance for main line running. It was the first time that a Southern 'U' had been over these routes since before 1967.

Below: No. 31625 at Westcott near Dorking on the Redhill to Reading line on 9th January 1999. These engines were synonymous with this route.

Above: 'Merchant Navy' Class Pacific No. 35005 *Canadian Pacific* joined main line duties under the ownership of Andrew Naish who restored it at the Great Central Railway. By this view at Wilton in March 1999, No. 35005 was owned by Steam Dreams and painted in the experimental blue livery more associated with its un-rebuilt form of the early 1950s.

Right: Canadian Pacific is seen at Salisbury on the return leg of its journey on 13th March 1999.

Standard Class 5 No. 73096 was another locomotive based at the Mid-Hants which entered the main line circuit. Running 'Day Light' tours based at Alresford became a part of the MHR business at the time. No. 73096 is seen at Tunnel Hill, Pirbright. This route was heavily used in 1966 for diverted trains avoiding the Bournemouth electrification work. 29th May 1999.

Above: Mid-Hants flagship engine No. 34016 *Bodmin* is seen at speed at Potbridge, near Winchfield on 30th August 2000. By now Cathedrals Express had taken over the Daylight tours once based at the MHR.

Right: No. 73096 at Littlehampton on 29th May 1999, one of many destinations covered by Daylight Tours.

Ivatt 2-6-2 tank No. 41312 was also registered to run on the main line following completion of its overhaul in 2000. It is seen, left, emerging from Tunnel Hill Pirbright on its return from working at the 'Steam on the Met' event in London.

Above: The engine is seen operating the *'March Hare' at* Badshot Lea on 26th March 2000.

Below: The return journey seen at the same location.

Above: No. 35005 *Canadian Pacific* at the well-known spot of Battledown flyover south of Basingstoke. The locomotive was by now (2000) owned by the Mid-Hants Railway Preservation Society and re-painted in more traditional Southern Region Brunswick green.

Right: Canadian Pacific about to depart from Warnford after a photographic stop whilst working The Cathedrals Express on 10th October 2001.

Above: No. 35005 at Weydon Lane, Farnham hauling one of the Cathedrals Express trains on 14th April 2002.

Left: Canadian Pacific at Enton Hall on Witley bank. The 'green train' was developed from a set of Mark 2 carriages especially for use on the southern-based Daylight trains.

Right: 'MN' No. 35005 passing Dinton station near Salisbury at speed. The train would be on its way towards Yeovil.

Below: Quite possibly the most dramatic photograph I have ever taken! *Canadian Pacific* heads west through Dinton on the south west main line from Salisbury. It was heading a train towards a raging storm with these dramatic lighting effects! The author just managed to get back to his car before the heavens opened! April 2002

Visiting engines

Above: GWR King Class No. 6024 *King Edward 1* was a visitor to the railway's Gala in May 2002. It passes by the Ropley up distant signal.

Left: Ivatt tank No. 41312 is coupled to visiting engine No. 80078 from the Swanage Railway. 29th October 2000.

Above: Not a regular engine at Medstead & Four Marks station in Southern days, but King Class *King Edward 1* makes a fine sight as it runs into the station from Alton on Gala day 4th May 2002.

Right: Another of the many visiting engines to come to the MHR is unique GWR No. 3440 *City of Truro*. This National Railway Museum locomotive was returned to steam in 2003 and has visited several times since. It was reputed to have achieved 103 miles per hour in 1903 down Wellington bank. Dave Wiseman Jnr is seen driving the unique engine at Alton.

Above: No. 45231 visited the railway as part of a Gala with *City of Truro* on 13th March 2005. The LMS Black Five heads *City of Truro* and *Bodmin* at Medstead.

Left: More associated with Hampshire is LSWR 'B4' dock tank No. 96 *Normandy.* Owned by the Bluebell Railway's Bulleid Society, this engine was once used in Southampton Docks and latterly at Corrells Coal depot in Northam, Southampton. It is seen entering the cattle dock at Alresford on 4th March 2006.

Above: No. 96 *Normandy* drifts down towards Alresford close to the old A31 road bridge during the railway's Spring Gala in March 2006. Many of the dock tanks had names from areas and places in northern France.

Right: The following year's Spring Gala in March 2007 saw another visitor from the Bluebell Railway. LBSCR 'E4' in its early BR livery as No. 32473. When in LBSCR colours it carries the name of *Birch Grove*.

Above: No. 32473 arrives at the delightful station of Medstead & Four Marks. The signalbox here was acquired from Wilton, just to the west of Salisbury.

Right: Another unique tank locomotive visited the line in March 2009. Here is Met No. 1 in its attractive maroon livery. It enters Medstead station during a Gala.

Above: 'Castle' Class No. 5029 *Nunney Castle* was a star guest at the Gala in September 2008.

Left: Beattie well tank No. 30585 and Met No. 1 together at Ropley station during the Gala in March 2009. Both locomotives were from the Buckingham Railway Centre at Quainton Road.

Above: A Urie 'S15' hard at work coupled tender to tender with No. 34016 *Bodmin*. No. 506 is in its wartime black livery as carried until its withdrawal for overhaul in 2001. The two locomotives storm up towards Ropley during the late autumn Gala of October 2000.

Left: Viewed from Sun Lane at Alresford, all seems quiet as No. 34016 *Bodmin* waits to depart for Ropley and beyond to Alton. 4th May 2002.

End of Southern Steam Commemorated

The Mid-Hants Railway has on occasions commemorated the end of steam on the Southern Region which occurred in July 1967. In 2007 our locomotives were presented in a way that portrayed the look of the Bulleids and Standards in those last weeks in 1967. Here, 'Merchant Navy' Class No. 35005 was given the number of No. 35008 *Orient Line* and *Bodmin* was stripped of its nameplates, a feature of the period. Standard '5' No. 73096 was given long-lost sister engine No. 73029's number.

The National Railway Museum's Southern Railway Maunsell-designed locomotive from 1926 was allocated to the Mid-Hants Railway from 2009. No. 850 *Lord Nelson* was stored out of use for many years until it was taken to Eastleigh for a full overhaul. No. 850 was re-dedicated by HRH The Princess Royal at Eastleigh in 2006 after which a period of running on the main line then brought it to the MHR. It is seen, left, operating near Medstead and above and below, at the Eastleigh 100 event held in 2009 where it had a starring role.

Above: What a line-up! The MHR's 'Merchant Navy' Class No. 35005 *Canadian Pacific*, although out of use, was taken to Eastleigh Works' 100th Anniversary event in May 2009. The 'Merchant' is seen flanked by two Bulleid light Pacifics Nos. 34070 *Manston* and 34028 *Eddystone*, both from the Swanage Railway.

Right: 'West Country' Class No. 34007 *Wadebridge* became part of the Mid-Hants fleet in 2008. *Wadebridge* is the oldest surviving Bulleid light Pacific dating from 1945. It is seen arriving at Ropley from the Medstead direction.

Restoration of 'Schools' Class No. 925 *Cheltenham* at Eastleigh

In October 2010 Southern 'Schools' Class No. 925 *Cheltenham* was given to the Mid-Hants on loan from the National Railway Museum. From York, the locomotive was taken into the works at Eastleigh where it was originally constructed in 1934, to be fully restored to working order again.

Above left: Cheltenham is towed from the former foundry building to the erecting shop to be completed. The old office block at Eastleigh is seen behind the locomotive.

Above: No. 925 within the erecting shop receiving its final coat of Southern green paint and gold lettering and lining out in May 2012.

Left: Fully restored, the locomotive's first public display was at York's Railfest event in June 2012.